Gatecrashed Lover

Gatecrashed Lover

A Musical

Nathan Silvers

authorHOUSE®

AuthorHouse™
1663 Liberty Drive
Bloomington, IN 47403
www.authorhouse.com
Phone: 1-800-839-8640

Published by AuthorHouse   04/23/2012

ISBN: 978-1-4567-9379-1 (sc)
ISBN: 978-1-4567-9667-9 (e)

Any people depicted in stock imagery provided by Thinkstock are models, and such images are being used for illustrative purposes only.
Certain stock imagery © Thinkstock.

This book is printed on acid-free paper.

SYNOPSIS

This is a tale about the life of **RACHEL ALBINIAN**; it shows how **RACHEL** only wants a 'normal' life, however many aspects of her lifestyle forbid this. This play tells us how she fights all obstacles in her way to get what she wants, eventually learning what it is she wants from life, she then chases her dream and begins to unravel the secrets of the "Gatecrashed Lover".

A note on the play

I began writing this play based on the idea of Cinderella, the idea came when I was in the garden of my family home.

I had just finished reading an amazing novel that was an inspiration to one of the best stage musicals ever produced, and I was amazed at how one story can change into several smaller ones.

I began to think how proud all of the producers in the world must be, whether film or theatre and I thought how fantastic it must feel to see one of your own pieces of written work performed on stage or screen.

As an aspiring Actor/Author I began to plot together a story for my first ever stage script, at first I thought it shouldn't be too hard to write a script for stage, which is where my dreams lie.

Working with a few ideas from my own imagination and combining them to ideas of my younger sister I began to form a plot for my new written piece, however a few weeks into the writing process I realised that I had left a few gaps so I went back and re-worked my piece.

I soon realised that my play was missing something but I couldn't put my mind on what it was, I asked my sister to read through what I'd written and to give me feedback. After reading it she merely said 'hmm', it was then that I discovered my sisters passion for song writing.

It was at that moment my new stage script took a rapid change from an adventure into a musical experiment and the idea of "Cinderella, The Musical" was born.

However later into the process yet again I thought there was something not quite right about my work and this time despite my happiness and pride that the script gave me,

I began to change the plot, it was then that I realised my problem, I knew that the well known fairy tale was an inspiration for my play and it was also barricading my ideas from flowing, so this time I decided to change most of the plot keeping only a few main points from the original tale of 'Cinderella'.

Within weeks I had almost finished the writing of my stage musical and I was fully happy with what I had achieved but there was one thing I felt didn't fit the context of my production, the title, this soon changed and the story of the 'Gatecrashed Lover' was born.

I hope you enjoy reading this production and I hope you enjoy travelling on the magical journey that I loved when writing it.

CHARACTERS

*RACHEL ALBINIAN the daughter of **EDWARD***

EDWARD ALBINIAN** the father of **RACHEL** and husband of **LARYNGIA

LARYNGIA CLEMENT** the mother of **BRIDGETT** and **BRIGHITTA**, **RACHEL**'s step mother and wife of **EDWARD

***BRIDGETT CLEMENT** the oldest twin sister, **BRIGHITTA**'s sister, **LARYNGIA**'s daughter*

***BRIGHITTA CLEMENT** the youngest twin sister, **BRIDGETT**'s sister, **LARYNGIA**'s daughter*

SERVANT** a **SERVANT** to **LARYNGIA

JOE CHARMIN** the son of **HOWARD**, friend of **PETE

HOWARD CHARMIN** father of **JOE**, friend of **EDWARD

MIA FELLEN** friend of **RACHEL

SALLY REGENT** friend of **BRIDGETT** and **BRIGHITTA

CHARLES PENN** a butler who works for **EDWARD** and **LARYNGIA

TED HEMMING** a chauffeur who works for **EDWARD** and **LARYNGIA

PETE** friend of **JOE

MESSENGER

A VICAR

A BEGGAR

Notes on the Characters

The characters within this production all have their own qualities and must be portrayed as a whole character.

RACHEL is a character who is not afraid to show how she feels she knows what she wants from life and will attempt anything to achieve it, the most important thing to *RACHEL* is her friends and family, this is portrayed within the character.

EDWARD is an elderly yet very physical man, he loves his family and friends, he is very emotional when thinking about life, *EDWARD* is also a very protective character who holds his family close to his heart.

LARYNGIA is portrayed in various ways throughout the play, at the beginning she is a very protective mother of *BRIDGETT* and *BRIGHITTA*, however a manipulative bitch to *RACHEL*. Further into the play *LARYNGIA*'s character starts to become very secretive and her behaviour begins to change and she becomes protective over *RACHEL*.

BRIDGETT is quite clearly the 'leader' of the *TWINS*, she is a sadistic manic character who will do anything to get what she wants, and she doesn't care who she hurts in the process, however throughout the play it seems *BRIDGETT* takes a 'back seat' and lets *BRIGHITTA* take over from her, knowing full well it will go wrong. *BRIDGETT* has a very strong stage presence and this is shown throughout.

BRIGHITTA can be labelled as the 'dumb twin' she never seems to understand what is going on but is keen to remain part of her sisters usually evil plans, *BRIGHITTA* admires her sister above anyone else and *BRIDGETT* knows this, *BRIGHITTA* wants to be just like her older sister and this should be shown.

The *TWINS* both have evil streaks within them which fade away during the production, however at the beginning they are both uncouth and dangerous and this must be shown.

The **SERVANT** is a character who hardly ever speaks although she is not shy and nor is she dumb, she is always around **LARYNGIA** and appears to be watching her; the **SERVANT** must be played like this as it is a huge clue to the ending of the production.

JOE is portrayed as a young teenager who like any other teenager wants to have fun, all of **JOE**'s lines alter in the way in which they must be said in act one his lines must be delivered with humour and slight childlike behavior, however in act two his lines become more serious because **JOE** realizes what he wants, however his lines can still be comic.

HOWARD is a simple jolly character. **HOWARD** is keen to have fun and enjoys having a laugh it should be quite clear he is the father of **JOE**.

MIA is a character who is not afraid to show her thoughts and feelings, she is very friendly and knows how to be a true friend, **MIA** is very protective over her friends and will do anything to protect them.

SALLY is like **MIA** in many ways however as she is a friend to the **TWINS** her idea of a true friend differs to **MIA**'s in several ways, **SALLY** believes that she is lucky to be friends with **BRIDGETT** and **BRIGHITTA**.

CHARLES should be portrayed as a very caring character who only wants the best for people in life, he has no family and his work means everything to him.

TED has similar characteristics to **CHARLES** as he too wants the best for people however **TED** also suffers from agitation and can be very impatient. He is a very caring gentleman.

PETE is the smallest role within this production although this does not make him less important, **PETE** should be portrayed as a very humorous young teenager who loves to be centre of attention. He is keen for fun and will do anything for a laugh, **PETE** is a very flirtatious character.

The **MESSENGER** is a simple character who works for anyone within the town, he often speaks without thinking.

The **VICAR** is a man of the Catholic Church and follows a strict belief of Christianity.

The **BEGGAR** is the simplest character within this production and must be portrayed quite simply as a **BEGGAR** who spends her life trying to take from other people sometimes resulting to theft.

Notes on the Production

The action of this production takes place in three main locations which are on stage throughout the performance, up stage right there is a table with three chairs around it, up stage centre there is a bed and bedside table, on which sits a lamp, up stage left is two blocks which represent a car.

The set is also used as various locations within the play, for example the edge of the table can be used as a wall within the grounds.

There are three main entrances for this production, stage left, stage right and an exit upstage.

All characters have an appointed place on stage, this is shown in act one, scene one.

Please Note: All stage directions given in this script are from the actors' point of view, stood centre stage facing the audience.

The Songs; Most songs in this production were written by Nathan Silvers. 'Charles's Song' were written by Hannah-Marie Silvers. 'True Love Tale' and 'The Destiny Song' were written by Nathan and Hannah-Marie Silvers.

The original casting of "*Gatecrashed Lover*" took place April 2009 with the cast as follows;

Director Nathan Silvers
Musical Director Sheldon Hulett
RACHEL ALBINIAN Sophie Danielle Yates
EDWARD ALBINIAN Matthew Watson
LARYNGIA CLEMENT Dawn Harris
BRIDGETT CLEMENT Nikita Yates
BRIGHITTA CLEMENT Hannah-Marie Silvers
SERVANT Emily Jayne Denton-Davies
JOE CHARMIN Dominic Turner
HOWARD CHARMIN Aidan Felis
MIA FELLEN Georgina Slack
SALLY REGENT Samantha Woodhouse
CHARLES PENN Damian Lomas
TED HEMMING Jacky Lam
PETE Jacky Lam
MESSENGER Aidan Felis
A VICAR Alexander Pountain
A BEGGAR Emily Jayne Denton-Davies

'However despite many attempts unfortunately the production of *Gatecrashed Lover* never took place. This production has never been performed'.

ACT ONE

Curtain rises; Lights up dim slowly; we see a table upstage right with three chairs around it; also upstage centre there is a bed with a bedside table beside it, on it is a lamp, upstage left is two blocks which represent a car.
***EDWARD** is sat on the bed alongside **LARYNGIA**, **BRIDGETT** is sat at the table on the chair on the right, **BRIGHITTA** on the left, **MIA** is stood behind the centre chair and **SALLY** is sat in front of the table, the **SERVANT** is stood in front of the drawers watching **LARYNGIA**, **CHARLES** and **TED** are sat on the blocks and **HOWARD** sits beside **CHARLES**, the **VICAR** is stood just left of centre stage, they are all frozen. **RACHEL** enters stage right, Lights up; she stands centre stage and begins to sing.*
THEY SING;
🎜**[SONG 1—'INTRODUCTION']**🎜

RACHEL

This is a story a tale of my life
A story that is true
Of how I became a wife
This is my tale that
I'm about to tell
I hope you enjoy it
And you like it well

It will begin at the start
And go on from there
And then at the end

3

I'm sure you will care

ALL CAST

We will tell you the story
As best as we can
We will tell you the tale
Of how it began
We will let your learn
The entire truth

Of all that happened
That long time ago

We will tell you the story
In our own little way
Tell you it all
And maybe you'll stay

We will tell you the story
As best as we can
We will tell you the tale
Of how it began

It is now the time to finish our song
Get on with the story
It won't take long

*RACHEL moves to the centre chair at the table, the **VICAR** turns to*
***EDWARD** and **LARYNGIA** he nods and steps aside left, **EDWARD** and*
***LARYNGIA** stand and place themselves centre stage holding hands, the*
***VICAR** stands behind them and looks to the audience.*
VICAR Dearly beloved we are gathered here today in the presence
of God to witness the marriage of ***EDWARD ALBINIAN*** and
LARYNGIA CLEMENT.
*We see the **VICAR** turn to **EDWARD** and **LARYNGIA**, he mimes talking*
*and we see **EDWARD** produce a ring and place it on **LARYNGIA'S** hand,*
*meanwhile **RACHEL** speaks.*

RACHEL He could have married anyone he wanted, but he chose Laryngia but I suppose it is his choice and I should be happy for him, after all that's what my mother would want, is it not?

VICAR I now pronounce you husband and wife, you may kiss the bride.

EDWARD and LARYNGIA lean in to kiss

RACHEL *[to MIA, covering her eyes];* I can't look

RACHEL and MIA laugh while the TWINS turn to look at them in disgust, Lights fade.

*RACHEL is sat in the centre chair at the table eating breakfast from a bowl, there is a cloth on the table along with 5 bowls, **TED** is sat on the first block stage left he is looking at the floor. **BRIDGETT** and **BRIGHITTA** enter stage right.*

RACHEL *[looking at them]*; Good Morning

BRIGHITTA *[grinning and walking to left side of the table]*; oh look Bridgett, Rachel has made you some breakfast

BRIDGETT *[grinning but standing on the right side of the table]*; aren't you kind, thanks **RACHEL**

> ***BRIDGETT** takes the bowl from **RACHEL** and sits down*

RACHEL *[standing up]*; B . . . But that's mine

BRIGHITTA *[also sitting down]*; not anymore it isn't

RACHEL *[trying to grab the bowl]*; But that's not fair

> ***RACHEL** continues to take the bowl from **BRIDGETT** but she keeps pulling away, **BRIDGETT** then stands up and throws the bowl on the floor where it tips over.*

BRIDGETT *[sarcastically]*; oops!

> ***RACHEL** looks upset, **BRIDGETT** and **BRIGHITTA** are laughing at her, **LARYNGIA** enters stage right*

LARYNGIA *[looking at the girls]*; what is happening in here?

> ***RACHEL** points at **BRIDGETT** and sees that **BRIDGETT** and **BRIGHITTA** are both pointing at her.*

BRIGHITTA Rachel threw it at Bridgett

> ***RACHEL** opens her mouth to say something but **LARYNGIA** cuts across her.*

6

LARYNGIA [To RACHEL]; Well you had better clean it up and quickly otherwise you are going to be late for school.

LARYNGIA exits right, BRIDGETT and BRIGHITTA walk towards the blocks where TED is now sat looking impatient, as the TWINS walk past RACHEL, BRIDGETT pushes RACHEL onto the floor, they pick her up and push her onto the blocks, they sit either side of her.

TED [turning to face them]; can you act sensibly while you are in the car please?

BRIGHITTA [with a snigger]; no

TED [angry]; then you can both get out of the car and walk; I'll drive only **RACHEL** from now on.

BRIDGETT [frowning]; will you? Then we'll see what our mum says about that shall we?

TED turns back around annoyed he begins to mime driving; there is the sound of an engine, a few seconds later the TWINS begin to push RACHEL again.

TED [impatient]; I have asked once can you behave while you are in the car please?

BRIDGETT [angry]; and we've told you once, no

TED [losing his temper]; When are you two going to learn, Rachel is your older sister and it is about time you treat her like one, one day you are going to need her and she won't be there for you.

BRIGHITTA [laughing]; oh please, need her, why would we ever need her, she's useless.

TED [furious]; right that is it, get out of my car now, I've had enough

BRIDGETT and **BRIGHITTA** *laugh.*

BRIDGETT make us

TED looks furious he then turns back around and drives with aggression muttering to himself. A few moments later he turns back round

TED [Outraged]; Out now!

BRIDGETT and BRIGHITTA laugh and get out from their side, BRIDGETT grabs RACHEL and pulls her onto the floor, and TED looks outraged.

Lights fade, **TED** *exits left, while* **RACHEL, BRIDGETT** *and*
BRIGHITTA *move centre stage,* **MIA** *enters stage right at the same time*
SALLY *enters left, Lights up;* **RACHEL** *is laying on the floor.*

MIA *[lifting* **RACHEL** *up];* Leave Rachel alone, she hasn't done anything
to you, pick on people your own size

SALLY *[looking at* **MIA** *and smiling];* you mean like . . . you?

MIA *looks at* **SALLY**, *she is stood with the* **TWINS** *who are both stood in
front of her with their arms folded.*

MIA *[defensively];* yeah, like me, leave Rachel alone she hasn't done
anything to you, leave her alone or I'll . . .

SALLY *[stepping forward];* you'll what?

MIA you'll be sorry

SALLY *[smirking];* is that a threat?

MIA *[menacing];* yes

SALLY *[turning to the* **TWINS**];* did you hear that, she's threatening us

BRIDGETT Yeah, we heard, she's just lucky we don't want to waste our
time on her

SALLY *[outraged];* what?

BRIGHITTA come on let's go

BRIDGETT, BRIGHITTA *and* **SALLY** *all start to exit stage right*
MIA *[watching them];* that's right and take your smell with you.

BRIDGETT *and* **BRIGHITTA** *stop,* **SALLY** *walks into them*

BRIGHITTA *[angry];* what did you just say to us?

MIA *[smiling];* I said take your smell with you

BRIGHITTA *[furious];* you what?

MIA *[laughing];* so you're deaf as well as stupid

SALLY *[outraged];* How dare you?

MIA *[sarcastically];* yeah I dare

SALLY *[stepping forward];* that it is it

BRIDGETT *[stepping forward and grabbing* **SALLY**];* leave them, they're
not worth it

BRIGHITTA *and* **SALLY** *exit right,* **BRIDGETT** *smiles.*

See you at home Rachel
> ***BRIDGETT*** *exits right,* ***MIA*** *turns to* ***RACHEL***

MIA I bet it is hell living with those two?

RACHEL not really
> *[Pause]*

Just when my fathers not around.
> *[Blackout]*

-3-

Lights come up, **RACHEL** *is sat on the bed writing on some paper using the drawer as a desk, there is paper cluttered over the bed. The* **TWINS** *enter from upstage, they creep towards* **RACHEL**.

BRIGHITTA *[shouting];* BOO!

RACHEL *jumps and her papers are scattered everywhere, the* **TWINS** *high five and begin to laugh,* **RACHEL** *is annoyed.*

RACHEL you could have just said hello?

BRIDGETT Where is the fun in that?

BRIGHITTA Anyway, Bridgett and I have been talking and we have decided that your room is bigger than ours.

RACHEL *[collecting the paper];* what do you mean, you have decided, it is quite obvious my room is bigger than yours is, you can't decide on a fact.

BRIDGETT Stop being so smart Rachel and listen to what we have to say

BRIGHITTA We've come to a decision that there is only one of you but two of us

RACHEL *[smirking];* Oh really and how long did it take you to realize that!

BRIGHITTA *opens her mouth in shock*

BRIDGETT shut up Rachel, what my dear sister is trying to say is that, we need a bigger room.

RACHEL *[confused];* so what has that got to do with me, tell dad and he'll rearrange one of the spare rooms for you

BRIDGETT *[smiling];* Oh no that won't be necessary

BRIGHITTA *[smirking];* we've already decided what room we want

RACHEL and what has that go to do with me, tell dad

BRIDGETT No you need to know that we're moving rooms

RACHEL *[sarcastically];* Why do I, are you too stupid and think you might get lost? Or do you need my help to move out?

BRIDGETT *[Smiling widely];* actually, it's the other way around

RACHEL *[confused];* what?

BRIGHITTA *[Slowly];* well you aren't going to help us move out, we're going to help you.

RACHEL What? What do you mean?

BRIDGETT well isn't it obvious? We want your room

RACHEL What, no this is my room, you can't have it.

BRIGHITTA We can, we're even going to help you move out.

> **BRIGHITTA** *grabs the chest of drawers and tips them over,* **RACHEL** *watches in horror while* **BRIDGETT** *is laughing,* **LARYNGIA** *then enters stage right.*

LARYNGIA what is going on in here?

> *Before anybody says anything,* **RACHEL** *speaks*

RACHEL *[pointing];* they want me to move rooms

> **LARYNGIA** *looks at the* **TWINS***, who are stood together looking at the floor,*

LARYNGIA what, is this true?

BRIGHITTA mum we want a bigger room, Rachel's is bigger than ours and there is only her in it, it's not fair.

BRIDGETT our room isn't big enough for us both mother.

LARYNGIA *[sternly];* I see, well then I'll talk to Edward and he can rearrange one of the spare rooms for you.

BRIDGETT *[interrupting];* But mum . . .

LARYNGIA *[sharply];* enough, I said I'd speak to **EDWARD** but in the meantime you all stay in your own rooms, do you understand me?

> **RACHEL** *smiles and the* **TWINS** *look upset,* **LARYNGIA** *turns to exit right she then stops and turns back*

And **RACHEL** pick up that paper, you might want to live in a dump but you're giving us a bad reputation!

*LARYNGIA exits, **RACHEL** is shocked, the **TWINS** are laughing. The **TWINS** go to leave in pursuit of their mother however as they leave **BRIDGETT** picks up the paper from the bed and throws it in the air.*
BRIDGETT Oops, sorry

*The **TWINS** exit, **RACHEL** sits on the bed and looks around, she sighs. Blackout.*

*Lights up; the **TWINS** and **SALLY** are sat talking on the back block stage right, **RACHEL** enters stage left followed by **TED**, and **RACHEL** is carrying her handbag.*
BRIGHITTA *[watching **RACHEL**]*; Oh no, Bridgett look, Rachel's here
BRIDGETT *[acting shocked]*; we're sorry Rachel we forgot about you and we accidentally invited Sally to ride with us, so there's no room in the car, I'm sorry.
*The **TWINS** and **SALLY** laugh, **RACHEL** looks unsurprised.*
RACHEL Oh dear, it looks like; I'll have to walk then.
*RACHEL turns around and exits stage left, the **TWINS** and **SALLY** look confused.*
Blackout

*Green light comes up; the **BEGGAR** is sat on the edge of the bed representing a park bench, she is playing with her fingers, **RACHEL** enters stage right, walking slowly across the stage.*
BEGGAR *[standing up]*; Hello dear, you couldn't spare some change for an old poor person could you?
RACHEL stops and takes her bag from her shoulders she starts to rummage inside
RACHEL Lets have a look
*RACHEL searches deeper within her bag while the **BEGGAR** watches intently, suddenly the **BEGGAR** takes the bag and starts to exit stage left at the same time **CHARLES** enters, the **BEGGAR** turn back to **RACHEL** and starts to laugh manically, she then runs into **CHARLES** and screams*
CHARLES *[sternly]*; I don't think that belongs to you does it?
*The **BEGGAR** screams again and runs off stage left; **CHARLES** picks up the bag and hands it to **RACHEL**.*

I think this belongs to you

RACHEL *[smiling and taking the bag];* Thanks Charles

[Pause]

What are you doing in the park anyway?

CHARLES oh I'm just taking a steady walk, where are you going?

RACHEL to school

CHARLES *[confused];* oh why didn't Ted take you?

RACHEL Bridgett and Brighitta invited Sally so there was no room in the car.

CHARLES oh I see, that sounds like them, I think its dreadful how they treat you and Ted agrees, we've seen them pushing you around and taking your things, they need to learn that you are their older sister and nothing they can do can change that, if they continue the way they are one day they will get what's coming to them.

RACHEL They aren't that bad, I've got used to them so I just ignore them most of the time

CHARLES but you are their older sister and they need to realize that, one day they may need you and you won't be there, they need to learn to accept you for who you are instead of bullying you for who you are not.

[Pause]

Now come on I'll walk to school with you and then when I get back I'm going to tell your father everything Ted and I have witnessed, there needs to be some change around the household otherwise the place will no longer seem home to any of us.

[Pause]

It's ever since Laryngia turned up she always seems to be around, and her Servant, she doesn't speak to anybody except Laryngia I saw them whispering together the other day and when Laryngia saw me watching she yelled at me to get out and do what I was paid for.

[Pause]

I think you are so lucky Rachel

RACHEL what? Why?

CHARLES well you are eighteen in a few weeks and then you can do what you want, in fact I've been thinking why don't you have an eighteenth party down in the cellar you can invite Mia and some other friends and if you keep it quiet nobody will know about it and you won't be disturbed, you can have yourself some 'you' time, what do you think?

RACHEL Yeah that sounds like a good idea, I'll ask dad to see what he says, thanks Charles.

*RACHEL exits stage left, **CHARLES** watches as soon as she disappears the grin fades from his face and he sighs, Light dim, **CHARLES** SINGS.*

♫[SONG 2—'CHARLES' SONG']♫

CHARLES

> There's something I really want to say
> But how do I break the news
> I've done this so many times before
> But still I've got no clues
>
> How do you say 'you are going to leave?'
> When you have been there for so many years
> A place that you have learnt to love
> And the people there are near
> Treating you like one of them, part of the family
>
> I've been in this house for many years
> It is a home to me
> Every time I think of it
> It brings back memories
> Of Sarah and Edward the day Rachel was born
> The day Sarah died was when things got torn
> And since that day, I have realised
> How much this place has changed?
> It has never been the same
> Never will again

Blackout

-4-

Lights up; **RACHEL** *and* **EDWARD** *are on stage they are sat at the table,* **RACHEL** *in the chair on the left while* **EDWARD** *is sat in the right, they have been discussing the party.*

RACHEL So?

EDWARD *[thoughtful];* well it sounds like a good idea to me honey, I could hire a karaoke as well if you like I know you love to sing, the number of times I woke up in the morning listening to you and Sarah singing together

[Pause]

Now all I hear is Bridgett and Brighitta with their attempt of singing *[EDWARD sighs];* Things have changed

[RACHEL laughs as the TWINS enter stage right]

BRIDGETT What are you two talking about?

RACHEL dad don't say-

EDWARD we we're just discussing having a party for Rachel's eighteenth-

BRIGHITTA A party?

BRIDGETT Why didn't you tell us?

RACHEL *[upset];* well it was going to be a surprise

BRIDGETT oh right well don't worry you can trust us

BRIDGETT exits stage left, BRIGHITTA looks confused but follows, RACHEL turns to her dad

RACHEL Dad I don't want them there, they are always ruining things and bullying me.

EDWARD Listen Rachel, they are you're younger sisters you have got to get used to them, I know it's difficult when you have been living as the only child for a while but now it's different

RACHEL *[Standing up];* But I don't want them there, I'm sick of them pushing me around like I have to listen to them, I've had enough of them and if you think they are going to keep my party a secret you're wrong it will be around the school tomorrow.

EDWARD *[sternly];* that's enough, I know you don't get on with your sisters but that's natural with a new family, I don't want you to talk about your sisters like that again, understand?

RACHEL *looks furious and she exits stage right,* **EDWARD** *stands and follows*

EDWARD Rachel?

The **TWINS** *then re-enter from upstage* **BRIDGETT** *is smiling* **BRIGHITTA** *looks confused*

BRIGHITTA Bridgett wait, what did you tell her she could trust us for? You know she can't.

BRIDGETT I know but I've got a plan that will make us seem trustworthy, at least for a while.

BRIGHITTA what?? I don't understand?

BRIDGETT My plan is going to make her seem popular but then when the time comes we will tell her the truth and she'll see how unpopular she really is.

BRIGHITTA I still don't understand?

BRIDGETT *[angry];* you never do?

THEY SING;

♫[SONG 3—'THE *TWINS* PLAN']♫

BRIDGETT

I have a plan that will work

Plan that will make her go berserk

A plan that is cruel

A plan that is fun

A plan that would work on anyone

BRIGHITTA

> Please tell me the secret
> Of your brilliant plan
> Tell me what is happening
> I don't understand

BRIDGETT

> Are you really that stupid?
> Or is it just an act?
> Why don't you learn?
> And then you can come back

BRIGHITTA

> I am trying to learn
> I want to understand
> Please can you tell me?
> What have you planned?

BRIDGETT

> Imagine we use posters
> And put them around the school
> Everyone will see them
> And think they are cool
> Imagine Rachel's face
> When people appear at our house
> Saying it's for her
> And they've come to hang about

BRIGHITTA

> Imagine Rachel's reaction
> When we tell her it's a joke
> Imagine what she'll do
> She'll shout and bust her throat?

BRIDGETT *[spoken];* you've got it
> *They continue singing*

Both

It is our time
To show our terror
Our time to prove forever
We don't like our sister
We think that she should suffer
It's time that we shown her
We don't need another

BRIDGETT

One sisters quite enough
I couldn't cope with another

BRIGHITTA

One sister is enough
And I don't want a brother

Both

It is our time
To show our terror
Our time to prove forever
We don't like our sister

We think that she should suffer
It's time that we show her
We don't need another

BRIDGETT [*spoken*]; so, are you interested?
BRIGHITTA yes, definitely

The **TWINS** *smile and high five, Lights dim and they move to the table and begin setting up dishes,* **RACHEL** *enters stage left and goes to sit in the centre chair,* **BRIGHITTA** *pulls it out for her,* **RACHEL** *is shocked*
RACHEL Thank you
BRIDGETT No problem, anything for our older sister, now what do you want for breakfast?
Blackout
Lights up; **RACHEL** *enters from stage right and walks across the stage* **MIA** *enters from upstage she is carrying a piece of paper*

MIA Hey Rachel wait!

RACHEL *[turning to face her];* oh hey Mia, how are you?

MIA *[suddenly];* yeah I'm ok, listen why you didn't tell me about your eighteenth party?

RACHEL *[shocked];* what, how do you know about that?

> **MIA** *shows* **RACHEL** *the poster and she looks outraged*

The little—Wait until I get my hands on them

> **RACHEL** *exits running stage left,* **MIA** *is confused but follows*

MIA Rachel Wait

> *Blackout*

Lights up; the **TWINS** *are sat on the edge of the table laughing;* **RACHEL** *enters followed by* **MIA** *stage left.*

RACHEL What do you think you are doing advertising my eighteenth around school?

BRIDGETT *[sarcastically];* Oh no you wanted it to be a secret didn't you, we're so sorry we were so excited about it, it must have . . . slipped our minds.

BRIGHITTA Besides you should be grateful.

RACHEL Grateful? Why should I, if I wanted to invite the whole school I would have done it myself?

> **LARYNGIA** *enters stage left followed by the* **SERVANT**

LARYNGIA What is happening in here?

MIA Bridgett and Brighitta have invited the entire school to Rachel's eighteenth.

LARYNGIA oh what a great idea

RACHEL No it's not I didn't want the entire school to come

LARYNGIA oh.

> *[Turning to face the* **TWINS***];*

In that case it was wrong of you

BRIDGETT We are sorry mum, we were only trying to help

LARYNGIA Well next time I suggest you leave it to Rachel after all she is so smart, however I think you should remove all the posters and tell everyone it's been cancelled, that way Rachel can invite her friends, although I'm sure she won't object to inviting Sally?

LARYNGIA exits upstage, the SERVANT stares at the TWINS for a few moments
BRIDGETT [snapping]; what are you looking at?
The SERVANT says nothing and follows LARYNGIA
Blackout

5

*There is party music playing and disco lights flashing, **RACHEL** and **MIA** are sat with arms folded on the edge of the table. The **TWINS** are stood centre stage with microphones they are miming to sing, **SALLY** is sat behind them on the edge of the bed with her fingers in her ears looking distraught. There is a loud crash and the music turns off, the lights are still flashing, everyone is looking around and we see **JOE** and **PETE** fall onto stage, stage left, they stand up and brush themselves down, they then look around*

PETE Hey isn't this a party?

*The music turns back on this time quiet, **PETE** walks to the **TWINS** and takes the microphones he throws them to **JOE** who puts them underneath the blocks stage left.*

PETE That's better, now

PETE *stands in between the **TWINS** and puts his arms around them both* So ladies tell me, what are your names?

*The **TWINS** look shocked and they turn towards **PETE** and start hitting him, he escapes from them and exits stage right*

PETE oops!

JOE *is laughing so is **RACHEL** and **MIA**, **JOE** looks around and then sits with **SALLY**, **SALLY** looks scared and walks off stage left. **JOE** looks confused he then sees **RACHEL** watching him, he looks at her and then he approaches her*

JOE *[holding out his hand];* Joe

      RACHEL *shakes his hand looking confused*

RACHEL Rachel

JOE smiles

JOE would Rachel like to dance?

RACHEL *looks at* **MIA** *who smiles and nods,* **RACHEL** *takes* **JOE'S** *hand and he leads her to centre stage, as they reach it a slow song begins to play, the music is louder again.*
While they dance a slow waltz we see **PETE** *enter from upstage he sees* **JOE** *and* **RACHEL** *and wolf whistles at them,* **MIA** *turns around and smiles at him, he sees her and walks to her taking her hand,* **PETE** *and* **MIA** *then begin to dance.*
RACHEL *and* **JOE** *continue to dance gradually getting closer together, they then move in closer and their eyes meet they move closer to one another and they lean in towards each other.*
BRIDGETT *and* **BRIGHITTA** *then enter stage right, they see* **PETE** *dancing with* **MIA** *and they start towards him when they see* **RACHEL** *and* **JOE** *kissing, they look horrified and run towards* **RACHEL** *pulling her from* **JOE**, **RACHEL** *looks shocked and* **JOE** *confused,* **MIA** *and* **PETE** *have stopped dancing and* **MIA** *is confused, the* **TWINS** *drag* **RACHEL** *off stage right and* **PETE** *stands with* **JOE**.
PETE time to leave?
JOE *looks at* **PETE** *and grins they then turn and exit stage left,* **MIA** *is shocked.*
Blackout

Lights up; **RACHEL** *flies from stage right and falls on the floor, the* **TWINS** *follow her, they both look livid as they stand around* **RACHEL**.
BRIDGETT What the hell do you think you were doing trying to ruin our party?
BRIGHITTA Yeah who gave you the right to do that?
RACHEL *[standing up];* what? Your party it was my eighteenth!
BRIDGETT So do you think that matters to us, wasn't it obvious we planned it to prove to you how unpopular you are, when we took down the posters and told people it was cancelled, how many people wanted to come when you asked them?
[Pause, **RACHEL** *is outraged]*
You see nobody wanted to come.

BRIGHITTA nobody likes you Rachel, they all think you're worthless and so do we.

*RACHEL grabs **BRIDGETT** and starts to pull her hair, **BRIDGETT** retaliates and starts to punch **RACHEL**, **BRIGHITTA** looks scared and exits stage right.*

*The **SERVANT** then enters right and sees **RACHEL** and BRIGDETT, she*
rushes forwards and pulls them from each other looking furious
SERVANT Don't you ever try and harm Rachel again otherwise . . .
BRIDGETT Otherwise what? What are you going to do?
   ***BRIDGETT** pushes the **SERVANT** as **LARYNGIA** enters stage right*
LARYNGIA [Outraged]; Bridgett what on earth do you think you are
   doing?
BRIDGETT *[looking shocked];* Mum she hit me
LARYNGIA She wouldn't dare, now get out
            ***BRIDGETT** goes to leave stage right but turns back*
BRIDGETT mum?
LARYNGIA I said go
                     [Calmly]
You too Rachel

***BRIDGETT** is outraged she storms off stage right **RACHEL** looks confused*
   *but follows, **LARYNGIA** approaches the **SERVANT** who smiles.*
SERVANT Well done, you should be proud
                     Blackout

*Lights up dim; **RACHEL** enters stage right at the same time as **JOE** enters stage left, they walk to the front and stand in two spotlights, they both look up.*
RACHEL Love
JOE Rachel

THEY SING;
♫[SONG 4—'THE DESTINY SONG']♫

RACHEL

> I never thought I would be the one to actually fall in love,
> But now I have actually done it, it feels really good

JOE

> I never thought I would be the one to give my heart away,
> But now I' have actually done it and I did it all today

RACHEL

> I never thought I would be the one
> The girl that is in his dreams

JOE

> But now it all so happens
> I was wrong it would seem

RACHEL

> I never knew it would be like this
> And things could be so great

JOE

> I never thought it would be me
> But I guess that is just fate
> *Blackout*

25

-8-

*Lights come up; **RACHEL** and **MIA** are sat on the bed together.*

RACHEL I've never felt this way before about anyone.

MIA *[smiling];* it's so great Rach I think you're in love.

RACHEL What, in love, no I can't be.

MIA You must be you haven't stopped talking about him for weeks, how did he make you feel when you were dancing together?

RACHEL I don't know, it was strange I felt tingly.

MIA you see you can't describe it; you're in love with him.

* **RACHEL** and **MIA** are laughing and **EDWARD** enters from stage right, looking upset*

RACHEL Hi dad

MIA Hey Mr. Albinian

EDWARD Rachel we've just had some bad news, we've just heard from a Messenger that Charles was found dead this morning, it appears he had a heart attack

RACHEL what?

EDWARD His funeral will be held next week

Blackout

-9-

Lights up; ALL CAST is on stage, there is a table placed downstage centre **HOWARD**, **EDWARD**, **TED** *and* **JOE** *walk from the upstage entrance carrying a coffin, the* **VICAR** *follows them, The CAST is in their allocated places as labelled in Act one scene one, when the coffin has been placed on the table,* **HOWARD** *and* **EDWARD** *stand in their places, while* **JOE** *sits next to* **HOWARD**.

VICAR Dear beloved we are gathered here today in the presence of god to witness the passing of Charles Penn.

Blackout

-10-

*Lights up; all cast members are still on stage, the coffin and table has been moved, the **VICAR** is stood talking to **HOWARD**, **EDWARD**, **TED** and **JOE** they are stood upstage left, meanwhile **LARYNGIA** and the **SERVANT** are stood the opposite side of the stage also talking, the **TWINS** are stood with **SALLY** in front of the drawers while **RACHEL** and **MIA** are stood centre stage, **JOE** walks away from the crowd and approaches **RACHEL**, she is crying, **JOE** hugs **RACHEL** and runs his hands through her hair, they break apart and **RACHEL** kisses **JOE** on the forehead.*

JOE We're having a barbeque next week and I'd like you to come

RACHEL I'd love to but I don't know where you live?

JOE *[pointing stage right];* through the forest with my dad

RACHEL your dad?

JOE Yeah *[he points to **HOWARD**];* my dad

RACHEL What Howard is your dad?

JOE well yeah, didn't you know?

RACHEL No, I mean Howard's known my dad for ages but I didn't know he had a son.

JOE Well he does and apparently he's gorgeous, but I have never seen him, have you?

RACHEL *[sarcastically];* No, but I'd like to see your brother

JOE What? Oh, *[laughing];* no I'm the only child

RACHEL oh I thought Howard's son was gorgeous?

Blackout

-11-

Green lights come up; **RACHEL** *and* **JOE** *are sat on the edge of the stage kissing,* **HOWARD** *enters from upstage he is about to speak when he sees them he smiles and exits again.*

JOE erm, what was that for?

RACHEL being you?

JOE oh erm, thanks for coming anyway

RACHEL It's been great maybe next time I could bring **MIA** and you can bring your friend.

JOE who?

RACHEL I don't know who he is, the person who came to my party with you?

JOE oh right, that's Pete *[laughing]*; I doubt I'll be able to bring him he's gone away for a while.

RACHEL oh *[pause]* and I've been meaning to ask you, how did you know about my party, it was only advertised around my school?

JOE *[laughing]*; exactly, it was only advertised around your school, so I knew

[RACHEL looks confused, JOE sighs]

I was walking past your school and I saw a poster on the floor

RACHEL oh, anyway I've got to go I'm sorry

RACHEL stands, **JOE** *does also,* **RACHEL** *kisses him on the cheek and then goes to exit stage right,* **JOE** *grabs her hand*

JOE Rachel, wait.

THEY SING;
♫[SONG 5—'DREAM COME TRUE']♫

JOE

> It would be a dream come true
> To spend more time with you

RACHEL

> It would be a thing so fine
> If you would be mine

JOE

> It would be a chance so great

RACHEL

> A chance that I would take

JOE

> I dream of the day
> To have someone like you

RACHEL

> I dream of the night
> I could spend with you
> I want this dream to come to life nothing else matters
> I would sacrifice

ALL CAST

> This is your chance
> To make it together
> This is your time to hold on forever

RACHEL

> This is my dream
> I want to come true

JOE

> This is my life
> I want to share with you

ALL CAST

It is your time
To make it right
It is your chance to shine

JOE

My chance to make it right
My chance to make you mine
They kiss
Blackout

-12-

*Lights up; **LARYNGIA** is sat at the table in the chair facing the audience; the **SERVANT** is stood behind her. The **TWINS** are also sat at the table, **BRIDGETT** on the right, **BRIGHITTA** on the left. **EDWARD** is pacing up and down, **RACHEL** enters stage right.*

LARYNGIA *[standing up]*; **RACHEL**, there you are, we were all starting to get worried

BRIDGETT *[running and embracing **RACHEL**]*; we're so happy you're home we didn't know where you had gone.

BRIGHITTA *[also running and embracing **RACHEL**]*; We searched all over for you but we couldn't find you.

RACHEL *[surprised and smiling]*; I only went to Joe's through the forest; I did tell you I was going to their barbeque today.

EDWARD Well that doesn't matter now, what does matter is that you are home and you are safe, so come on it is bed time.

***EDWARD** pulls the **TWINS** from **RACHEL** and he hugs her himself, he slowly lets go and kisses her forehead*

Come on, it has been a long day, everyone to bed.

***EDWARD** exits stage right, followed by **BRIDGETT** and **BRIGHITTA**, **RACHEL** looks at **LARYNGIA** and smiles she then starts to exit in pursuit of the others.*

LARYNGIA *[standing up]*; Rachel?

***RACHEL** turns*

Are you sure you are ok? We were all so worried when we discovered you had gone.

RACHEL Yes I'm ok, I'm just feeling tired, goodnight.

RACHEL exits right, LARYNGIA sighs and walks to the front of the table,
the SERVANT watches.
THEY SING;
♫[SONG 6—'*LARYNGIA*'S SONG']♫

LARYNGIA

Life has changed so much for me
I have come so far in so little time
I never thought that I would be this happy
Never thought that I would be set free
But now I know my time is coming
The end is near I fear

This happiness will come to stop
And my whole life will fail
I have lived and loved my entire life
I have thought so hard
I have sacrificed
I have built my life from scratch

I have been a success
But now it's cracked

Life is not what it was
Life is not just a job
Life could be so great
Life could humiliate
But now I see a different light
A husband, children
My future looked bright

I'd give myself to let it grow
Give up the world
To let them know
I love them all
But it does not show

LARYNGIA & SERVANT

Life has changed so much for me
I have come so far in so little time
I never thought that I would be this happy
Never thought that I would be set free
But now I know my time is coming
The end is near I fear
Blackout

-13-

Lights up; **RACHEL** *is sat in bed reading,* **BRIGHITTA** *can be heard offstage;*

BRIGHITTA *[offstage];* Rachel?

   RACHEL *looks around looking for the voice*

RACHEL *[uncertain];* Hello?

 BRIGHITTA *enters upstage, and sits on the edge of the bed,* **RACHEL** *places her book down and watched her, there is silence.*

RACHEL erm, Brighitta what are you doing in my room?

BRIGHITTA oh, *[she looks nervous]* I wanted to apologise

RACHEL *[confused]* what for?

BRIGHITTA *[looking at the floor]* for being nasty to you all the time, I . . .

       [Pause]

I was thinking today when we couldn't find you and I realised that you are my older sister and I should look up to you and respect you even if you are a little weird . . . I just wanted to say sorry and that from now on I'll try and be a better sister.

RACHEL *[surprised];* oh, thanks Brighitta, I really don't know what to say.

BRIGHITTA Well you could start by accepting my apology

RACHEL *[laughing];* oh right, yeah of course I do

BRIGHITTA Thank you

   BRIGHITTA *starts to leave upstage but turns back,*

BRIGHITTA Bridgett wanted me to apologise for her too because she's too stubborn to admit she's sorry but I know she is, Goodnight
RACHEL
    BRIGHITTA *exits upstage,* **RACHEL** *smiles and lays down*
        Blackout.

*Lights up; the **TWINS** are stood centre left, **SALLY** is stood centre right, they all look furious*

SALLY Fine if that's how you feel go and find your precious sister and hang around with her because there is no way I'm hanging around with that cow, besides I don't need you I have plenty more friends.

*   **BRIDGETT** grabs **SALLY** and starts to pull her hair, **BRIGHITTA** screams and starts to kick them both, **BRIDGETT** releases **SALLY**.

SALLY Don't you ever talk to me again.

*SALLY exits stage left, the **TWINS** watch*

BRIGHITTA go! We don't need you anyway, WE'VE got plenty more friends

*   **BRIGHITTA** looks at **BRIDGETT** smiling, **BRIDGETT** looks serious, they look at each other for a few seconds and then the grin fades from *
BRIGHITTA

BRIGHITTA we haven't have we?

BRIDGETT walks downstage right
THEY SING;
♫**[SONG 7—'THE *TWINS* SONG']**♫

BRIDGETT

I did not think I would lose a friend

BRIGHITTA

I would not think this is the end

BRIDGETT

I did not believe it would be like this

BRIGHITTA

I do not understand this little twist

BRIDGETT

Sometimes things happen you can not explain

BRIGHITTA

That happens to me, again and again

Both

I am not sure why this happened to us
We have been friends forever

BRIGHITTA

Since we were cubs

BRIDGETT

I am not sure why this is the end

Both

But do not forget that we are still friends
Blackout

-15-

Lights up; ALL CAST are stood in their allocated places, **SALLY** *is absent.*

BRIDGETT and so we told her that if she wasn't going to be nice to Rachel we didn't want to speak to her again

BRIGHITTA and she ran off crying

BRIDGETT and then later we saw her in detention

BRIGHITTA we heard that she had kicked a table and she's also got to pay for the damage

RACHEL so then she found me and told me what had happened

MIA we all laughed so much that we had to let them walk with us, then Sally saw us all together later and she ran off crying.

They laugh

I've always wondered what it would be like to have a pair of sisters and now I want a pair of my own.

They all laugh again.

EDWARD *[looking around at everyone];* Well isn't this nice, a happy ending

LARYNGIA *[smiling];* my favorite endings

SERVANT Well it isn't over yet.

RACHEL That's true.

THEY SING;

♫[SONG 8—FINALE SONG, ACT ONE]♫

RACHEL

It is only half a story that has been told

JOE

HOWARD

> Only half a tale that has been sold

TED

> It's not over yet for it has just begun

ALL

> Not over yet—now let us have fun

EDWARD

> This is a tale about our different lives

LARYNGIA

> How each is different

> How each one survives

ALL

> For this is a tale and it is so true
> We could not have done it
> Without the help of you

BRIGHITTA

> I have learnt new ways
> And I have met new friends

MIA

> Friends beside you until the end

BRIDGETT

> I have learnt I am different
> And I can be good

MIA

> Better and kinder like a sister should

LARYNGIA

> I have got a new family
> And it feels so great

EDWARD

> Got a new family
> And found a new mate

ALL

> This is a tale about our different lives

RACHEL

How each is same

JOE

How each feels right

ALL

For this is a tale and it is so true
We could not have done it
Without the help of you

RACHEL

I have got good sisters
And I have fell in love

JOE

I have a girlfriend, aren't I good?

TED

I have done new things
And I am in with the crowd

HOWARD

Got close to my son—I feel so proud

ALL

But this tale is half over
It's nearly done

SERVANT

Oh, how it has changed
Since it begun

ALL

But it is not over
We have got half the rest
The tales not finished
Now here's
The
Rest . . . . .

Blackout

CURTAIN CLOSE

ACT TWO

-1-

Curtain rises; Lights come up; **RACHEL, MIA, SALLY, BRIDGETT** *and* **BRIGHITTA** *are all on stage.* **RACHEL** *is sat in the centre chair at the table with* **MIA** *stood behind her,* **BRIDGETT** *is sat on the left while* **BRIGHITTA** *sits on the right,* **SALLY** *is stood stage right in front of the table talking to them.*

SALLY I just wanted to apologise I've been stupid and I know what I said was wrong, that is why I am here I wanted to put it right.

BRIDGETT we did wonder how long it would take you.

BRIGHITTA we knew you wasn't going to just walk out on us.

RACHEL Well it's good of you to come and apologise.

MIA although it was horrible what you said to us.

SALLY I know but I really am sorry, I want another chance please?

RACHEL I don't know, Mia?

MIA I'm not sure, Bridgett?

BRIDGETT I . . . I, what do you think Brighitta?

BRIGHITTA of what?

RACHEL Should we give Sally another chance or not?

BRIGHITTA another chance to what?

BRIDGETT haven't you been listening to anything, Sally's been asking for another chance to be our friend and we're trying to reach a decision

BRIGHITTA well I hope she's apologised

SALLY [**SALLY** *sounds distressed,* **BRIGHITTA** *jumps at hearing her voice];* of course I've apologised, now have you reached a decision or not.

MIA taking that tone won't help anything.

SALLY sorry.

RACHEL that's better now decision time.

MIA *leans into* **RACHEL**, *while* **BRIDGETT** *and* **BRIGHITTA** *lean in, they have a whispered conversation,* **SALLY** *watches nervously.*

BRIDGETT ok, *[turning to* **SALLY**]*;* you have one chance, ruin it and it's over for good this time.

SALLY ok, thank you so much.

Blackout

-2-

Lights up; **EDWARD** *and* **JOE** *enter stage right*

EDWARD Rachel is upstairs; I'll just go and get her for you.

JOE Thank you.

    EDWARD *exits upstage,* **JOE** *turns around and looks around,*
LARYNGIA *enters from upstage carrying a washing basket, she walks to the table and places it down,* **JOE** *doesn't notice her.*

LARYNGIA *[***JOE*** jumps at the sound of her voice and spins around to face her, he screams]* Hello?

    JOE *looks at* **LARYNGIA** *who stares at him he screams again*
That is not a reaction I have ever had before.

JOE err . . . Sorry?

LARYNGIA *[Laughing];* It's ok.

        RACHEL *enters upstage*

RACHEL Hi, what are you doing here?

    JOE *looks nervously at* **LARYNGIA**, *she watches them while they spoke*

JOE Erm I just wondered if you wanted to walk into town and erm . . .

LARYNGIA *[grinning];* talk?

JOE yeah erm talk . . . thanks

        LARYNGIA *picks up her basket and exits upstage*

RACHEL yeah, that sounds great, thank you

           Lights fade dim

-3-

JOE and *RACHEL* *are sat on the edge of the stage, green light is shown*

RACHEL so how are you?

JOE Oh I'm ok, thanks,

[urgently]; listen Rachel I need to tell you something

RACHEL oh, ok what is it?

JOE *[he sighs];* Well can you remember when we first met?

RACHEL *[laughing];* yes of course I can you gate crashed my eighteenth

JOE *[more urgently now];* yeah I know well after I left I felt like, I felt that . . .

[he sighs]

Look I can't describe it, I . . . I

[JOE stands up, RACHEL does too]

I'm sorry

JOE goes to exit stage left, RACHEL grabs him

RACHEL Joe Don't go, what is it you want to tell me? Just tell me, please

JOE turns to RACHEL and looks upset, he turns and looks at RACHEL, he then sighs. JOE walks back to RACHEL and holds out his hands she takes them.

THEY SING;

♫[SONG 9—'TRUE LOVE TALE']♫

JOE

When we first met there's something that I needed to say

RACHEL

48

When we first met
I wish I didn't go away

JOE

When you had gone
I felt that I had something to do

RACHEL

While I was gone all I could think of was you

Both

Now we're here
Me and you

RACHEL

Look into my eyes

JOE

Say you feel it too

RACHEL

I'm in your arms

Both

By your side

JOE

Whatever people do

Both

There's a chance we'll make it through

RACHEL

Now we're together we're never gonna be apart

JOE

Together forever
I'm never gonna break your heart

RACHEL

Now I see you're the only one that's right for me

JOE

Together forever that is what we'll always be

Both

Now we're here
Me and you

RACHEL

Look into my eyes

JOE

Say you feel it too

RACHEL

I'm in your arms

Both

By your side

JOE

Whatever people do

Both

There's a chance we'll make it through
There's a chance we'll make it through

ALL CAST

There's a chance we'll make it through
There's a chance we'll make it through

Blackout

-4-

*Lights up dim, a plaque is shown that reads 'four years later', lights Fade. Lights up; **LARYNGIA**, **TED** and the **TWINS** are stood stage right; **RACHEL** is sat at the table on the chair on the right. **EDWARD** is sat on the chair on the left.*

LARYNGIA We should be back by midnight but depending on how Mavis is feeling depends on how long we'll stay, I'll see you later

*   **LARYNGIA** kisses **EDWARD** and he stands up, **LARYNGIA** and the TWINS then exit stage right following **TED**.*

EDWARD Well that's them gone, just me and you, anything you want to do?

*   There is a knocking sound, **EDWARD** stands up*

I'll get it

*   **EDWARD** exits stage right, **RACHEL** stands up, **MESSENGER'S** voice can be heard before he enters stage right led by **EDWARD**, the MESSENGER sees **RACHEL** and pauses.*

EDWARD Rachel, that message was for you.

MESSENGER It reads

*   [pulling out a scroll and reading from it];*

"Dear Rachel please meet me at the town hall at the ninth chime of the clock tonight, thank you, Love, your Joe PS please wear something as beautiful as you, if that is possible which I very much doubt"

RACHEL *[looking at **EDWARD**];* Why does he want me to meet him at the town hall?

EDWARD I've got no idea, but you should go and get ready otherwise you will be late

51

*RACHEL nods and exits upstage as the **MESSENGER** exits right,*
***EDWARD** watches **RACHEL** leave, he then sits in the centre chair.*
HE SINGS;

♫[SONG 10—'OUR LIVES']♫

EDWARD

> Life has changed so much for me
> I have come so far in so little time
> I never thought that I would be this happy
> Never thought that I would be set free
> But now I know my time is coming
> The end is near I fear

EDWARD sighs and exits stage right, lights fade and then rise again,
RACHEL enters upstage wearing a beautiful dress, she approaches the bed
*and looks underneath. **RACHEL** pulls out a box which she places on the*
bed, she slowly takes off the lid and pulls out a pair of silver shoes, she sits on
*the bed and looks at them, **EDWARD** enters from upstage.*

EDWARD oh look at you, you look stunning and

> *[EDWARD notices the shoes];*

Those shoes, they . . .

RACHEL I know, the last present mum ever got me before she . . .

EDWARD Sarah?

*EDWARD sits on the bed and puts his head in his hands, **RACHEL** hugs*
*him she slowly puts the shoes on, **RACHEL** then kisses **EDWARD** and exits*
*upstage, **TED** and **HOWARD** then enter stage right, they sit at the table,*
***HOWARD** sits on the chair on the left, **TED** on the right. **EDWARD** sees*
them he wipes his face and then moves to sit on the centre chair.
THEY SING;

♫[SONG 11—'OUR LIVES REPRISE']♫

EDWARD

> Life has changed so much for me
> I have come so far in so little time
> I never thought that I would be this happy
> Never thought that I would be set free
> But now I know my time is coming
> The end is near I fear

HOWARD

I know life can be hard
And sometimes seem quite bad
But believe me I know It gets better
I know it is not always sad

TED

Life can be better
It is not the way it seems
Think of what you have got
And what you have seen

ALL

Our lives our lucky
Our lives are great
Our lives could be better
And that's no mistake
Our lives are not the worse
Neither are they the best
But our lives
Are worth living
And we're glad we are not dead

They look at each other and laugh, **HOWARD** *stands and exits stage right,*
TED *also stands and starts to follow as he does,* **EDWARD** *coughs, he turns*
back, **EDWARD** *smiles at him,* **TED** *turns back and goes to leave again,*
EDWARD *then faints onto the table,* **TED** *comes rushing back*
TED Ed? Ed?
Blackout

-5-

Lights up; **JOE** *is stood centre stage wearing a suit,* **RACHEL** *enters from stage left and he holds out his arm, she takes it and they kiss.*
RACHEL What did you want to meet me here for?
JOE *[smiling];* You'll see

       JOE *leads her off stage left*

-6-

Waltz music is being played, lights are flashing, **JOE** *and* **RACHEL** *enter from upstage.*

RACHEL *[looking around];* wow, a ball.

JOE *[smiling];* I thought you would like it.

   JOE *spins* **RACHEL** *into himself and grabs her other hand, a slow song begins to play they dance throughout the song, at the end of the song, they break apart and kiss,* **JOE** *lets go of her hand.*

JOE I'll be back in a minute

   JOE *exits upstage,* **RACHEL** *watches and then sits on the edge of the table. Blackout.*

Lights up; **JOE** *enters from upstage he walks centre stage and wipes his face as though he is looking into a mirror, he wipes his face again.*
HE SINGS;

♫[SONG 12—'FOREVER MINE']♫

JOE

It is time in my life to make a choice
I know I finally understand
I know what it is I must do
For it is now that it is planned

It is my duty to do this
To face my task ahead

I know this is what I want
And that is why I've said

It is time to move forward
It is time to make things right
It is time to focus
On my dreams in the night

This is what I want
For my dreams to come true
All that I dream is to have you

ALL CAST

It is time to move on
It is time to go up
It is time to progress
Not mess things up
You know what to do
For it's already planned
It is in your pocket
For her hand

JOE

Forever in my heart
Forever in my dreams
Forever by my side
Forever my queen

JOE *then reaches into his pocket and pulls out a ring box he opens it and*
smiles.
Blackout

-8-

Waltz music is being played, **RACHEL** *is sat on the edge of the table,* **MESSENGER** *enters stage right holding a scroll he hands it to* **RACHEL** *and stands waiting,* **RACHEL** *reads the scroll and she starts to cry, the* MESENGER *taps her on the shoulder and exits stage right,* **JOE** *appears at the upstage entrance as he enters,* **RACHEL** *stands up and exits running stage left,* **JOE** *looks confused.*

JOE Rachel?

> **JOE** *exits stage left in pursuit of* **RACHEL**
> *Blackout*

-9-

*Lights up; **LARYNGIA** is sat on the centre chair at the table while **BRIDGETT** is sat on the left while **BRIGHITTA** remains on the right, **RACHEL** enters stage right, **LARYNGIA** stands up and rushes towards her they hug as **JOE** enters stage right, he notices everyone is crying and remains motionless.*
Blackout.

-10-

*Lights up; ALL CAST are in there allocated places exempt **JOE**, **HOWARD** and **TED**. The table is also back on stage, The **VICAR** enters stage right and stands facing the upstage exit, he stands next to the table centre stage. **JOE**, **HOWARD** and **TED** enter carrying a coffin, **TED** is at the front while **JOE** and **HOWARD** support the back, **JOE** is stood on the left while **HOWARD** is on the right. They reach the table and place the coffin down, they then move to their places looking at the floor, the **VICAR** turns around.*

VICAR Dearly beloved we are gathered here today in the presence of god to witness the passing of Edward Albinian, a loving father and husband.
Blackout

-11-

*Lights up; **LARYNGIA** is sat on the centre chair at the table, **RACHEL** is sat on the chair on the left while **MIA** sits on the right, **BRIDGETT**, **BRIGHITTA** and **SALLY** are all sat in front of the table, **BRIDGETT** is sat far right with **SALLY** in the middle. The **SERVANT** is stood behind **LARYNGIA**, they are all very tearful, The **SERVANT** is facing away from everyone.*

RACHEL I am going to miss him so much.

BRIDGETT I know me too.

BRIGHITTA I didn't even know him that well but I feel like-?

MIA There's something missing.

SALLY It doesn't seem right.

RACHEL The world doesn't seem as big anymore.

LARYNGIA I know how you all feel, but Edward would not want us to sit around grieving he would want us to continue life and be happy, I just think Edwards's death couldn't have been a worse time.

RACHEL What do you mean a worse time? Dad didn't want to die

LARYNGIA I know that, I just mean

[Pause]

Well last night when you went to the ball with Joe, he was going to propose to you, your father knew what was going to happen and he didn't believe that his little girl had finally grown up but he felt that if you were to marry Joe, he would lose you.

60

RACHEL *[shocked];* Joe was going to ask me to marry him?

LARYNGIA *nods,* **RACHEL** *stands up*

RACHEL I need to find him

RACHEL *exits stage right*

Blackout

-12-

Lights up; **RACHEL** *is sat on the end of the bed she looks stressed,* **LARYNGIA** *enters from upstage.*

LARYNGIA did you find him?

RACHEL no I looked everywhere he could have been but I couldn't find him

LARYNGIA hugs RACHEL

LARYNGIA Well I'm sure he'll turn up somewhere; did you go to his house?

RACHEL yes but he wasn't there and his dad said he hadn't seen him since the funeral yesterday, he could be anywhere

LARYNGIA I'm sure he'll be ok though dear, you just get some rest and I'll see you later ok, keep your chin up.

They hug and then **LARYNGIA** *exits upstage,* **RACHEL** *lays down and we hear a knocking sound,* **RACHEL** *jumps from her bed and looks around scared*

RACHEL Hello?

JOE slides out from underneath RACHEL'S bed and looks up at her, **RACHEL** *smiles*

JOE erm, Hi?

RACHEL *[smiling];* I've been looking for you

JOE *[sitting up];* Yeah I couldn't help hearing

RACHEL Well I wanted to know what you wanted.

JOE *[confused, standing up];* What do you mean?

RACHEL *[grinning];* the other night at the ball, you wanted to say something didn't you?

JOE looks confused

Or was it ask?

JOE looks horrified

JOE Oh right, that was no big deal, it doesn't matter, besides your dad was more important.

RACHEL Yeah he was, but I suppose what you wanted to say or ask can't be that important to you otherwise you would have already asked or said, wouldn't you?

RACHEL smirks and JOE looks at the floor

I'm going out into the garden, just in case you need me

RACHEL exits upstage, JOE watches and then looks around himself, he pulls out the ring and looks upset he looks to where RACHEL exit and sighs

Blackout

-13-

Green light comes up; **RACHEL** *is sat on the edge of the table, she is sat watching the sky,* **JOE** *enters from stage left he sees her and freezes watching her*

JOE *[nervously];* Rachel?

   RACHEL *looks at him and smiles, he approaches her and takes her hands*
I did and still do have something to say to you, and If I don't say it soon I never will, what I need to say means a lot to me and it is rather important, well to me anyway.

RACHEL *[standing up];* go on then

JOE *[he sighs and looks at her];* Well We have known each other for four years now and whenever I'm with you I feel the world is right, I feel

   [Pause]
As if I am a better person when I'm with you and you make me feel like no one ever has before

   [Pause]
I love you Rachel and I though that instead of trying to let fate intervene I would try and create a future for myself.

   [Pause]
A future where I'm the happiest man in the world and the only way, that is possible is if you are beside me every step of the way.

   [Pause]
From the moment we met at your eighteenth and I looked into your eyes and I knew you were the one person I wanted to spend the rest of my life with, you still are the only person I want to spend my life with

and I feel that you will always be there for me, I feel that without you in my life, it wouldn't be worth living.

[Pause]

RACHEL I love you and you mean everything to me, I know I will never stop loving you.

JOE lets go of RACHEL'S hands and bends on one knee pulling the ring box from his pocket, he opens it and shows RACHEL she looks overwhelmed So I ask, Rachel Albinian will you do me the great honour and privilege of becoming my wife?

Lights dim, there is a spotlight on JOE and RACHEL, RACHEL smiles and takes the ring, JOE looks up at her, RACHEL then takes JOE'S hand he looks confused.

THEY SING;

♪[SONG 13—'FOREVER MINE, REPRISE']♪

RACHEL

It is time in my life to make a choice
I know I finally understand
I know what it is I must do
For it is now that it is planned

JOE

It is time to move on
It is time to go up
It is time to progress
Not mess things up

BOTH

Forever in my heart
Forever in my dreams
Forever by my side
Kings and Queens

-14-

Lights dim, **RACHEL** *and* **JOE** *kiss while all the CHARACTERS enter the stage and stand in their allocated places.* **RACHEL** *and* **JOE** *break apart and hold hands facing the audience, The* **VICAR** *enters stage right and stands in front of them facing them.*

VICAR Dearly beloved we are gathered here today in the presence of god to join these two souls together in holy matrimony, welcome to the marriage of Rachel Albinian and Joe Charmin.

Blackout

Lights up; ALL CAST are on stage in their allocated places, except **RACHEL** *and* **JOE**, *they are all frozen,* **RACHEL** *enters stage right, followed by* **JOE**, **RACHEL** *stands centre stage.*

RACHEL and so we come to the end of my story, the story of the Gatecrashed Lover, as you can see it ends just how it began, with a marriage, although several changes have been made throughout my story, but take a look at what there is here.

A happy family, everyone here is important in some way, I just hope we can all live happily ever after but thinking back it turns out that the answer behind it all is love, it would turn out that love can change anything, even if it is unexpected.

THEY SING;
♫[SONG 14—'FINALE SONG']♫

RACHEL

This was a story a tale of my life
A story that was true
Of how I became a wife
This was my tale that
I've just told
I hope you enjoyed it
And you liked it well

It began at the start
And went on from there
And then at the end
I'm sure you did care

ALL CAST

We have told you the story
As best as we can
We have told you the tale
Of how it began
We have let you learn
The entire truth

Of all that happened
That long time ago
We have told you the story
In our own little way
Told it you all
Told it today

We have told you the story
As best as we can
We have told you the tale
Of how it began

It is now the time
To finish our show
Get on with our lives
And watch our kids grow

I hope you enjoyed
Please show your applause
The story is now over
As it has been before

Blackout

-15-

*Lights come up; it is an empty stage, The **SERVANT** enters stage left, she walks to the table and sits on the edge of it.*

SERVANT Many years ago, I was approached by Sarah Albinian who informed me she was dying, she insisted that as the town witch it was my job to help her, Sarah told me she wasn't afraid of death and would be happy to embrace it when the time came, However she wanted me to carry out a mission in her memory.

Sarah told me that she wanted her family to be kept safe and happy, she instructed me to look after her husband Edward and her only child, Rachel, a few weeks later Sarah died.

It was then I began to begin my journey to carry out Sarah's wish, after months of work, I had learnt that the only way to keep an eye on the family was to place people within their household, so I then began my plan, in a few short weeks I had managed to track down two small children who had decided to run away from their homes, I bewitched them and gave them a completely new memory.

It was then I began to work on my most advanced piece of witchcraft, I decided to transform my most beloved crow into the children's mother, I instructed my crow to remain in the house and keep an eye on the family, only when the family was safe and happy would my crow be released. Although as a precaution I decided to follow my crow and work within their presence.

LARYNGIA *enters upstage and walks centre stage, she kneels down. The* **SERVANT** *watches her.*

LARYNGIA I have done what I was asked, Sarah's family is safe and happy, I have done what I promised it is now your turn to honour our agreement.

*The **SERVANT** nods*

RELEASE ME

*The **SERVANT** nods again*

RELEASE ME

Lights fade; the sound of flapping wings and a crow cawing is heard, there is a scream and the crow caws loudly.

Blackout

CURTAIN CLOSE

ACKNOWLEDGEMENTS

Within these acknowledgements are the names of several people who have influenced me or helped me with this process however no matter what is written about individual people I would like to note every single name within these pages is extremely important.

Firstly I would like to thank my parents for their continued love, support and encouragement gave by them, during not only this process but for everything that I have ever done or attempted to do. Travelling on this journey has proved to me a lesson well learnt by many characters in my play;

"Family and friends are more important than you can ever imagine and love certainly is the most powerful thing to possess".

I would also like to mention all of the support I have been gave by hundreds of people in my life, to name but a few who have had the greatest impact upon the process, Jonathon Francis; who helped me greatly throughout the entire rehearsal process, Diane and Derrick Hulett; who gave much needed constructive criticism on my work and thousands of useful tips on improving it, Florence Cheesman; who encouraged me to never give up, all of the students attending a performing arts course at Chesterfield College during the years 2008-2010; who supported me greatly and also the lecturers who worked there; I couldn't have achieved my dream if you didn't believe in me.

Nathan Silvers

Throughout the entire process of my production I met so many wonderful people and each of them are important to me in their own special way I would also like to thank; Kelsey Cotterell, Amy Walton, Carrie Johnson, Kelsey Stirling, Natalie Lee, Grace Bissell, Thomas Vernon and Liam Bluff.

Every person who is mentioned in my acknowledgements I feel have shown me a gift that they should be proud of, however despite my previous thanks, my next set of names in my opinion are the most important people of all.

Each name below is written because they are my closest friends who I feel have travelled down the very same journey as I, they have found the bumps and curves of the road and also hit a few troubles but together we have broke through, without these people I know the production would never have been complete, it is these people that make me who I am and I couldn't love them anymore, this special thanks goes to;

Liam Bluff, Adam Chapman, Hannah Elshaw, Aidan Felis, Sheldon Hulett, Michaela Jeffs, Jacky Lam, Alex Pountain, Hannah—Marie Silvers, Georgina Slack, Kelsey Stirling, Dominic Turner, Matthew Watson, Andrew Witham, Samantha Woodhouse, Nikita Yates, Sophie Yates and Richard Zsirai.

I am extremely grateful to Elise Walton and Sarah Button, both of whom had a great input within the editing process of my script, I couldn't live without either.

A final thanks goes to my entire family, wherever you may be you are in my heart.

Finally to all who appear on these pages, my heart goes to you and you shall remain implanted within my soul, I love you.

Nathan Silvers